242.8 PRAYER, MEDITATION
CLASS   1911
                                           ACC

Stevenson, Robert Louis
(LAST NAME OF AUTHOR)

Prayers Written at
(BOOK TITLE) Vailima

DATE DUE	ISSUED TO

242.8
Ste_____   1911
        CLASS   ACC.

PRAYER, MEDITATION

Stevenson, Robert Louis
(LAST NAME OF AUTHOR)

Prayers
(BOOK TITLE)
Written at Vailima

PRAYERS

Decorations and calligraphy
by Hilda Scott

PRAYERS

Written at Vailima
by Robert Louis Stevenson

The Macmillan Company
New York – 1960

THE INTRODUCTION
by Mrs. R. L. Stevenson

In every Samoan household the day is closed with prayer and the singing of hymns. The omission of this sacred duty would indicate, not only a lack of religious training in the house chief, but a shameless disregard of all that is reputable in Samoan social life. No doubt, to many, the evening service is no more than a duty fulfilled. The child who says his prayer at his mother's knee can have no real conception of the meaning of the words he lisps so readily, yet he goes to

his little bed with a sense of heavenly
protection that he would miss were the
prayer forgotten. The average Samoan
is but a larger child in most things,
and would lay an uneasy head on his
wooden pillow if he had not joined,
even perfunctorily, in the evening
service.

With my husband, prayer, the direct
appeal, was a necessity. When he was
happy he felt impelled to offer thanks
for that undeserved joy; when in sorrow, or pain, to call for strength to
bear what must be borne.

Vailima lay up some three miles of continual rise from Apia, and more than half that distance from the nearest village. It was a long way for a tired man to walk down every evening with the sole purpose of joining in family worship; and the road through the bush was dark, and, to the Samoan imagination, beset with supernatural terrors. Wherefore, as soon as our household had fallen into a regular routine, and the bonds of Samoan family life began to draw us more closely together, Tusitala felt the necessity of including our retainers in our evening devotions. I suppose ours was the only white man's family in all Samoa, except those of the missionaries, where the day naturally ended with this homely, patriarchal custom. Not only were the religious scruples of the natives satisfied, but, what we did not foresee, our own respectability –and incidentally that of our retainers –became assured, and the influence of Tusitala increased tenfold.

After all work and meals were finished, the "pu," or war conch, was sounded from the back veranda and the front, so that

it might be heard by all. I don't think
it ever occurred to us that there was any
incongruity in the use of the war conch
for the peaceful invitation to prayer.
In response to its summons the white
members of the family took their usual
places in one end of the large hall, while
the Samoans—men, women, and children—trooped in through all the open
doors, some carrying lanterns if the
evening were dark, all moving quietly
and dropping with Samoan decorum
in a wide semicircle on the floor beneath
a great lamp that hung from the ceil-
ing. The service began by my son read-

ing a chapter from the Samoan Bible, Iusitala following with a prayer in English, sometimes impromptu, but more often from the notes in this little book, interpolating or changing with the circumstances of the day. Then came the singing of one or more hymns in the native tongue, and the recitation in concert of the Lord's Prayer, also in Samoan. Many of these hymns were set to ancient tunes, very wild and warlike, and strangely at variance with the missionary words.

Sometimes a passing band of hostile warriors, with blackened faces, would peer in at us through the open windows, and often we were forced to pause until the strangely savage, monotonous noise of the native drums had ceased; but no Samoan, nor, J trust, white person, changed his reverent attitude. Once J remember a look of surprised dismay crossing the countenance of Tusitala when my son, contrary to his usual custom of reading the next chapter following that of yesterday, turned back the leaves of his Bible to find a chapter fiercely denunciatory, and only too applicable to the foreign dictators of distracted Samoa. On another occasion the chief himself brought the service to a sudden check. He had just learned of the treacherous conduct of one in whom he had every reason to trust. That evening the prayer seemed unusually short and formal. As the singing stopped he arose abruptly and left the room. I hastened after him, fearing some sudden illness. "What is it?" I asked. "It is this," was the reply; "I am not yet fit to say, 'Forgive us our trespasses as we forgive those who trespass against us.'"

It is with natural reluctance that I touch upon the last prayer of my husband's life. Many have supposed that he showed, in the wording of this prayer, that he had some premonition of his approaching death. I am sure he had no such premonition. It was I who told the assembled family that I felt an impending disaster approaching nearer and nearer. Any Scot will understand that my statement was received seriously. It could not be, we thought, that danger threatened anyone within the house; but Mr. Graham Balfour, my

husband's cousin, very near and dear
to us, was away on a perilous cruise.
Our fears followed the various vessels,
more or less unseaworthy, in which
he was making his way from island
to island to the atoll where the exiled
king, Mataafa, was at that time im-
prisoned. In my husband's last
prayer, the night before his death,
he asked that we should be given
strength to bear the loss of this dear
friend, should such a sorrow befall us.

PRAYERS

FOR SUCCESS

Lord, behold our family here assembled.
We thank Thee for this place in which
we dwell; for the love that unites us;
for the peace accorded us this day; for
the hope with which we expect the
morrow: for the health, the work, the
food, and the bright skies, that make
our lives delightful; for our friends in
all parts of the earth, and our friendly
helpers in this foreign isle. Let peace
abound in our small company. Purge
out of every heart the lurking grudge.
Give us grace and strength to forbear

and to persevere. Offenders, give us the grace to accept and to forgive offenders. Forgetful ourselves, help us to bear cheerfully the forgetfulness of others. Give us courage and gaiety and the quiet mind. Spare to us our friends, soften to us our enemies. Bless us, if it may be, in all our innocent endeavours. If it may not, give us the strength to encounter that which is to come, that we be brave in peril, constant in tribulation, temperate in wrath, and in all changes of fortune, and, down to the gates of death, loyal and loving one to another. As the clay to the potter, as the windmill to the

wind, as children of their sire, we
beseech of Thee this help and mercy
for Christ's sake. ❧

FOR GRACE

Grant that we here before Thee may be set free from the fear of vicissitude and the fear of death, may finish what remains before us of our course without dishonour to ourselves or hurt to others, and, when the day comes, may die in peace. Deliver us from fear and favour: from mean hopes and cheap pleasures. Have mercy on each in his deficiency; let him be not cast down; support the stumbling on the way, and give at last rest to the weary.

AT MORNING

The day returns and brings us the petty round of irritating concerns and duties. Help us to play the man, help us to perform them with laughter and kind faces, let cheerfulness abound with industry. Give us to go blithely on our business all this day, bring us to our resting beds weary and content and undishonoured, and grant us in the end the gift of sleep.

EVENING

We come before Thee, O Lord, in the end of thy day with thanksgiving.

Our beloved in the far parts of the earth, those who are now beginning the labours of the day what time we end them, and those with whom the sun now stands at the point of noon, bless, help, console, and prosper them.

Our guard is relieved, the service of the day is over, and the hour come to rest. We resign into thy hands our sleeping bodies, our cold hearths, and open doors. Give us to awake

with smiles, give us to labour smiling.
As the sun returns in the east, so let
our patience be renewed with dawn;
as the sun lightens the world, so let
our loving-kindness make bright
this house of our habitation. ⁊

ANOTHER FOR EVENING

Lord, receive our supplications for this house, family, and country. Protect the innocent, restrain the greedy and the treacherous, lead us out of our tribulation into a quiet land.

Look down upon ourselves and upon our absent dear ones. Help us and them; prolong our days in peace and honour. Give us health, food, bright weather, and light hearts. In what we meditate of evil, frustrate our will; in what of good, further our endeavours. Cause injuries to be forgot and benefits to be remembered.

Let us lie down without fear and awake and arise with exaltation. For his sake, in whose words we now conclude. ⌘

IN TIME OF RAIN

We thank Thee, Lord, for the glory of the late days and the excellent face of thy sun. We thank Thee for good news received. We thank Thee for the pleasures we have enjoyed and for those we have been able to confer. And now, when the clouds gather and the rain impends over the forest and our house, permit us not to be cast down; let us not lose the savour of past mercies and past pleasures; but, like the voice of a bird singing in the rain, let grateful memory survive in the hour of darkness. If there be in front of us any painful duty, strengthen us with the grace of courage; if any act of mercy, teach us tenderness and patience. ∾

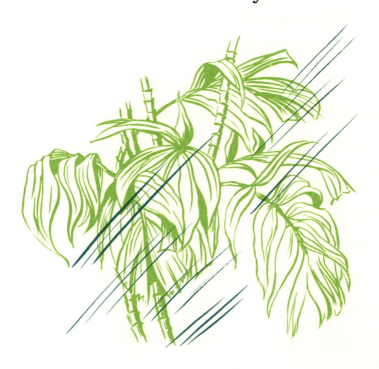

ANOTHER
IN TIME OF RAIN

Lord, Thou sendest down rain upon the uncounted millions of the forest, and givest the trees to drink exceedingly. We are here upon this isle a few handfuls of men, and how many myriads upon myriads of stalwart trees! Teach us the lesson of the trees. The sea around us, which this rain recruits, teems with the race of fish; teach us, Lord, the meaning of the fishes. Let us see ourselves for what we are, one out of the countless number of the clans of thy handiwork.[3] When we would despair, let us remember that these also please and serve Thee.

BEFORE A
TEMPORARY SEPARATION

Today we go forth separate, some of
us to pleasure, some of us to worship,
some upon duty. Go with us, our
guide and angel; hold thou before us
in our divided paths the mark of
our low calling, still to be true to
what small best we can attain to.
Help us in that, our maker, the dis-
penser of events – Thou, of the vast
designs, in which we blindly labour,
suffer us to be so far constant to ourselves and our beloved.

FOR FRIENDS

For our absent loved ones we implore thy loving-kindness. Keep them in life, keep them in growing honour; and for us, grant that we remain worthy of their love. For Christ's sake, let not our beloved blush for us, nor we for them. Grant us but that, and grant us courage to endure lesser ills unshaken, and to accept death, loss, and disappointment as it were straws upon the tide of life.

FOR THE FAMILY

Aid us, if it be thy will, in our concerns.
Have mercy on this land and innocent
people. Help them who this day contend
in disappointment with their frailties.
Bless our family, bless our forest home,
bless our island helpers. Thou who hast
made for us this place of ease and hope,
accept and inflame our gratitude; help
us to repay, in service one to another,
the debt of thine unmerited benefits
and mercies, so that, when the period
of our stewardship draws to a conclusion,
when the windows begin to be darkened,

when the bond of the family is to be loosed, there shall be no bitterness of remorse in our farewells. ❧

*H*elp us to look back on the long way that Thou hast brought us, on the long days in which we have been served, not according to our deserts, but our desires; on the pit and the miry clay, the blackness of despair, the horror of misconduct, from which our feet have been plucked out. For our sins forgiven or prevented, for our shame unpublished, we bless and thank Thee, O God. Help us yet again and ever. So order events, so strengthen our frailty, as that day by day we shall come before Thee with this song of gratitude, and in the end we be dismissed with honour. In their weakness and their fear, the vessels of thy handiwork so pray to Thee, so praise Thee. Amen.

SUNDAY

We beseech Thee, Lord, to behold us with favour, folk of many families and nations gathered together in the peace of this roof, weak men and women subsisting under the covert of thy patience. Be patient still; suffer us yet awhile longer;–with our broken purposes of good, with our idle endeavours against evil, suffer us awhile longer to endure, and (if it may be) help us to do better. Bless to us our extraordinary mercies; if the day come when these must be taken, brace us to play the man under affliction. Be with our friends, be with ourselves. Go with each of us to rest; if any awake, temper to them the dark hours of watching; and when the day returns, return to us, our sun and comforter, and call us up with morning faces and with morning hearts—eager to labour—eager to be happy, if happiness shall be our portion—and if the day be marked for sorrow, strong to endure it.

We thank Thee and praise Thee; and in the words of him to whom this day is sacred, close our oblation.

FOR SELF-BLAME

Lord, enlighten us to see the beam that is in our own eye, and blind us to the mote that is in our brother's.

Let us feel our offences with our hands, make them great and bright before us like the sun, make us eat them and drink them for our diet. Blind us to the offences of our beloved, cleanse them from our memories, take them out of our mouths for ever. Let all here before Thee carry and measure with the false balances of love, and be in their own eyes and in all conjunctures the most guilty. Help us at

the same time with the grace of courage,
that we be none of us cast down when
we sit lamenting amid the ruins of
our happiness or our integrity: touch us
with fire from the altar, that we may
be up and doing to rebuild our city: in
the name and by the method of him
in whose words of prayer we now conclude.

FOR SELF-FORGETFULNESS

Lord, the creatures of thy hand, thy disinherited children, come before Thee with their incoherent wishes and regrets: Children we are, children we shall be, till our mother the earth hath fed upon our bones. Accept us, correct us, guide us, thy guilty innocents. Dry our vain tears, wipe out our vain resentments, help our yet vainer efforts. If there be any here, sulking as children will, deal with and enlighten him. Make it day about that person, so that he shall see himself and be ashamed. Make it heaven about him,

Lord, by the only way to heaven, forgetfulness of self, and make it day about
his neighbours, so that they shall help,
not hinder him.

FOR RENEWAL OF JOY

We are evil, O God, and help us to see it and amend. We are good, and help us to be better. Look down upon thy servants with a patient eye, even as Thou sendest sun and rain; look down, call upon the dry bones, quicken, enliven; recreate in us the soul of service, the spirit of peace; renew in us the sense of joy.

Here end the Prayers of
Robert Louis Stevenson
as designed, written out, and
decorated by Hilda Scott;
reproduced for
The Macmillan Company.
New York — 1960